Looking Good, Feeling Good

Dr. Barbara Becker Holstein

ISBN: 978-1-7367862-8-4

Copyright © 2023 by Dr. Barbara Becker Holstein

All rights reserved.

No portion of this book may be reproduced in any form without written permission from the publisher or author, except as permitted by U.S. copyright law.

Contents

Introductions   V

1. Looking Good, Feeling Good   1
2. Freedom   7
3. More Freedom And Fun   13
4. Grown-ups Have Stuff to Learn   19
5. More Parents Should Learn   25
6. I'm Smart   31
7. I Know So Much   37
8. My Feelings Were Hurt   43
9. Mr. Reid Saves The Day   49
10. Just Me Can Be Good Enough   55
11. My Future   61
12. Wisdom   67
13. I Have A Lot of Courage   73
14. The Best Day Ever   79
15. Worried About Who I Will Marry   85
16. Dancing   91

About Dr. Barbara Becker Holstein   93

Also By Dr. Barbara Becker Holstein   95

Introductions

Hi there, I'm Angela! I'm a 12-year-old girl and I've discovered something really important. I've found this really cool way to feel good no matter what happens. You won't believe it, but **asking the right**

questions and writing down the answers has made such a big difference in how I feel about myself and how I handle challenges. It's like having my own secret power to navigate through all the ups and downs of life. I love spending time in my room, jotting down my thoughts and discoveries in my special notebook. It's become my little haven of self-reflection and growth.

Life has its ups and downs, but with my trusty questions and a notebook by my side, I'm ready to take on whatever comes my way! It might sound a little strange, but it totally works for me! So, if you're ever curious about how to feel stronger and more confident, just learn to look inside, ask the right questions, and you might find the answers . . . (don't forget to write them down!)

I hope my short episodes about myself and the questions I jotted down to get a better sense of who I am and what is important to me, get you going to explore yourself. Feel free to answer the three questions I pose after each episode in my life or take episodes from your own life and write them down and then also write the questions and thoughts that come to your mind as you process understanding and dealing with whatever has happened in your life. Don't be surprised to discover that if you take events from your life you have begun to not only to keep a type of diary but you are also telling the important stories of your life, of who you are, what is important to you and how you solve the problems that face you.

I'll share some episodes and stories in my life to get your started, and plenty of space to write down your questions and answers as you either ponder events and feelings in my life or jump into stories and episodes in your life.

From Dr. Holstein:

She's here! The girl from the past. I'm so glad she could make it and get through all the mess we have created with social media and loneliness and bullying and anxiety to give girls of today insight on how to handle life. As a positive psychologist, working with girls and women every day on resiliency, courage, their potential and dreams, I approve of her advice and courage.

Chapter One

Looking Good, Feeling Good

Sometimes, I stand in front of the bathroom mirror and look at myself. When I do that, I feel pretty. I have "dirty" blond hair and brown eyes. My teeth are a little crooked, and I have a space between my top two front teeth, but my mother says that makes my smile interesting. I have nice hands. They look good in the mirror, too. I enjoy looking at myself. Sometimes I hold up my hands in the mirror like I'm in a commercial selling nail polish. I just kind of smile at myself and hold my hand up so the nails show, and my eyes just shine. Then I move my hand a little, like models do on TV. I really feel special when I'm doing this. I know the truth about looks: The most important thing is to feel pretty. If you feel pretty, then you look pretty. That is the truth for me.

What makes me special?

What am I proud of about myself?

What special qualities do others see in me?

LOOKING GOOD, FEELING GOOD 3

LOOKING GOOD, FEELING GOOD

Chapter Two

Freedom

Here's what I do all by myself. I catch the bus two blocks from my house and go downtown. I'm not afraid. My mother said to sit near the driver, and I did. I talk to him sometimes. Other times I read. Today, going downtown, I read the saddest part of Little House on the Prairie.

The Ingalls' dog turned around three times and then lay down in his bed and died. I cried on the bus. I was glad I had a handkerchief with me. The driver asked if I was OK, and I told him the book made me sad because the dog died. He smiled in a kind way. When I got downtown, I bought some lace for a new doll's dress I am making, and I got an ice cream sundae in the diner. This time I got marshmallow sauce instead of whipped cream. I talked to the waitress I like, and I had a great time.

What do I want to learn or explore as I get older?
How can I make a positive impact in the world?
How does having more freedom make me feel?

LOOKING GOOD, FEELING GOOD

LOOKING GOOD, FEELING GOOD

Chapter Three

More Freedom And Fun

Next, I went to the dollar store. I looked at the makeup. The store has two aisles just filled with lipsticks, mascara, nail polish, and lots of other things for women. I had such a good time. I never get bored. A store like the dollar store is great because if I get tired of one section, I can always find a dozen more sections to wander around in. And they have a bathroom, which is very important. Then I waited for the bus to go home, and when it came, guess what? It was the same driver! I was so happy. I sat near him again. I'm so glad I can do things by myself. I feel so grown up. I don't think grown-ups understand how important it is to do things on your own and not be treated like a baby. I know what I'm doing, and I have a brain. I'm lucky my mom and dad let me do a lot on my own.

What new responsibilities have I taken on?

However I handle decisions on my own, what beliefs are important to me as I grow up?

LOOKING GOOD, FEELING GOOD

DR. BARBARA BECKER HOLSTEIN

LOOKING GOOD, FEELING GOOD

Chapter Four

Grown-ups Have Stuff to Learn

Last night, my parents had a big fight. I could sort of hear them through the walls of my room. I shut my eyes tight, but my ears were

wide open, like elephant ears, trying to hear every word. I couldn't, but they made me nervous, and I couldn't sleep. Today at school, I was exhausted. I'm the one who ends up worrying, with my heart pounding so loud I keep thinking it is going to pop out of my chest. They are the grown-ups. They shouldn't have stupid fights that keep their child awake. And anyway, nothing gets solved. No one feels better after he is yelled at or put down. No one is going to co-operate any better just because you yell at them and tell them all the things they do are wrong. Even I know that! And besides, they ruined my sleep. That isn't very nice for parents to do to a kid.

How can I help my parents when I think they need help?
What helps me take care of myself?
What are my strengths and coping skills?

LOOKING GOOD, FEELING GOOD

LOOKING GOOD, FEELING GOOD

Chapter Five

More Parents Should Learn

I should've been able to fall asleep and have sweet dreams! I know that too! I could teach my mom and dad so much, if only they would listen. Why would a grown-up put down someone he's supposed to love? I don't get it. They waste so much time fighting, and before you know it, everyone's mood is sad or angry and the day is ruined. This is one thing I'm really promising myself not to do when I grow up. Here is my recipe for happiness: Hug in the morning, hug at night, plan fun times that both agree upon, listen to your kids. My dad says, "Don't make a mountain out of a molehill." Well, even though he forgets his own words, I'm going to remember them, cause that is what is right.

How can I express my feelings to my parents?

What are some of my strengths my parents should know about?

How can I make my under my parents understand certain things?

LOOKING GOOD, FEELING GOOD

Chapter Six

I'm Smart

    I know I am very smart! Smart people solve mysteries and add numbers fast and realize if someone is lying. So, I know I'm smart. And that's the truth. I read my mom's copies of Nancy Drew Mysteries when it's raining out, and I have nothing to do. I've solved lots of them

BEFORE Nancy Drew does. Some of the Nancy Drew Mysteries I solved before Nancy solved them: 1. The Scarlet Slipper Mystery (two chapters before Nancy solved it) 2. The Ringmaster's Secret (the page before she solved it) 3. The Clue of The Velvet Mask (three chapters earlier!) 4. The Mystery at the Ski Jump (same page but first!) 5. The Clue of The Black Keys (five pages earlier) 6. The Secret of The Wooden Lady (I forget) 7. The Clue of The Leaning Chimney (about seven pages).

What are some of the topics or subjects a truly fascinate me?
How have I overcome challenges in learning at times?
What skills have I developed that make me feel proud?

LOOKING GOOD, FEELING GOOD

Chapter Seven

I Know So Much

A list of things I know how to do (list not finished): I know how to clean the house. I know how to do the laundry. I know how to cut and make doll clothing from patterns and design outfits for them even without a pattern. I have a special way to cut the tops for their clothes, so all I have to do is sew a snap and they stay on! I know how to tidy up the house. I know how to cook. I know how to use the microwave. I know how to draw. I know how to get into the house with the combination. I know how to read hard books. I know how to play the piano and make up music on the black keys, even though I never took any lessons. I know how to raise a lot of children; maybe even a dozen, like in Cheaper by the Dozen. I've read a lot of books about bringing up kids. Also, I am very loving and very good with people and animals. I can ride my bike for hours and go really fast downhill. I can rollerblade and ice-skate. I can do somersaults and bend over backwards. I can dance and make up steps. If you don't have a list of what you can do, make one. It helps make you feel smart.

How have I learned new skills in the past?

What are some ways I solve problems or approach tasks?

What can I learn or explore to expand my knowledge?

LOOKING GOOD, FEELING GOOD

LOOKING GOOD, FEELING GOOD

Chapter Eight

My Feelings Were Hurt

Today, my feelings were hurt. I raise my hand a lot in class. I have so many questions to ask. Miss Shannon was talking about the wheel and how it changed so many things in the world when it was invented. I raised my hand and asked what the world might have been like if something else had been invented instead of the wheel. She just looked at me with her really sharp grey eyes and said, "Now, isn't that silly!" Then she turned to everyone else and asked them to think of other inventions that depend on the wheel. It bothers me that Miss Shannon doesn't like my questions. Sometimes, she doesn't call on me at all, and I know she sees my hand waving. That makes me feel bad inside. But I don't give up, even if I have a funny feeling around my heart when she ignores me. I still raise my hand the next time I have a question.

What are some things I like about myself even if I felt hurt?

How can I make the best out of a difficult experience?

How can I remember to not define myself by someone else's reaction to me?

LOOKING GOOD, FEELING GOOD

Chapter Nine

Mr. Reid Saves The Day

These last few weeks of school have been wonderful. Guess why? Miss Shannon got sick, and we have the greatest substitute. His name is Mr. Reid, and he's fun and also nice. He told us he just finished becoming a teacher. I can't believe how different school has been. We made butter from milk by churning it by hand and we had crackers and butter. We made candles with real string and melted wax. He brought us all jump ropes and taught us how to exercise outside. He has a rule that we can't play anything where we choose sides until the last kid is chosen. CAUSE IT HURTS FEELINGS! He actually said that. I love him. And he always calls on me when my hand is up. Five times he told me what a great answer I gave. Three times he said the question I asked were terrific. I am feeling so good! Goodbye, Miss Shannon. I will never forget you, Mr. Reid!

What specific achievements in my most proud of?
How have I improved over time in certain areas?
What new challenges am I excited to take on?

LOOKING GOOD, FEELING GOOD

Chapter Ten

Just Me Can Be Good Enough

I know the truth about friends. Some people make you feel creepy, and they always make you feel bad. You shouldn't hang around with them. Some people make you feel wonderful. My best friend Gloria makes me feel good just by being with her. Dorothy makes me feel good also, but sometimes she gives me a little dig, and then I don't hang out with her for a while. This is what I suggest: If you don't have anyone good to hang out with, hang out with yourself, because you really understand yourself.

What qualities do I think my friends value in me?
Am I treating all my friends with kindness?
How can I let a friend know if she's mean to me?

LOOKING GOOD, FEELING GOOD

Chapter Eleven

My Future

I don't want to stay home during the day when I grow up. I'm going to really be somebody when I'm older. I'm not going to let anybody trap me inside a house with nothing to do but chores and laundry. I'll get the right education. If I'm going to be an actress, then I'll get that training. If I'm going to be something else, I'll do whatever it takes. I'm not going to be outside with the clothes basket hanging the clothes. My kids can hang the wash while I do more important things. I'm going to be somebody. And that's my Truth.

What is my dream for the future?

What steps can I take today to move closer to my dream?

What skills do I already possess that will help me build my future?

LOOKING GOOD, FEELING GOOD

Chapter Twelve

Wisdom

Grown-ups say they know so much more about life than kids do, but I know more lots of times. I know swearing is bad for all of us, bullying hurts, teasing mostly hurts, scary stories interfere with my sleep, and lots more. Here are some more: My parents fighting so I can hear them, my brother hiding my book I'm in the middle of reading, or eating the last piece of fudge I hid for myself. These can hurt.

What can I learn from bad situations?

How can I be positive during tough times?

How should I act when someone treats me badly?

LOOKING GOOD, FEELING GOOD

Chapter Thirteen

I Have A Lot of Courage

I have a lot of courage. I don't mind talking to strangers. Of course, I know when not to! Here is an example of when it is ok. I was with my mom in the Big Top restaurant, and I saw my dad's boss and walked up to him. I held out my hand to shake his, and he took it and said, "I'm so happy you came over to say hello to me!" He looked to see if I was with anyone. I pointed to my mom, and he walked me over to her. You know what he said to my mom?

"Do you know what a bright, friendly child you have?" My mom smiled ear to ear. And I was so happy with myself. My heart was beating so fast, and I know when I'm a grown-up, I will be brave and daring and not afraid to meet people.

What are some things that I'm proud of about myself?
How can I can step out of my comfort zone if I need to?
What brave action or actions can I take if and when I need to?

LOOKING GOOD, FEELING GOOD 75

Chapter Fourteen

The Best Day Ever

Today was the best day ever. My father took us on one of our mystery rides. I love them. No fighting allowed. We close our eyes until he tells us to open them. Then he drives around, and by the time he tells us to open them, we are somewhere we didn't expect to be like a new ice-cream parlor or a car dealership. Or a park where we like to walk around. My dad is amazing. I guess he is smart about a lot of things, like family fun. We have never gone to the same place twice. When I grow up, I'll do this same game with my kids.

What new discoveries have I made that I'm proud of?
How can I share what I've learned about the world?
What things in the world am I excited to explore next?

LOOKING GOOD, FEELING GOOD

Chapter Fifteen

Worried About Who I Will Marry

Speaking of growing up: Sometimes, I get worried about how I will know who to marry. I don't want to be alone as a grown-up. I want lots of people around me that care about me, and I care about them. And yes, I do want children. I know many people don't. That's okay, but I want at least four kids and two dogs, three cats, a bird that talks, and maybe a horse. So, the question is: who will I find to marry that has all the same interests? Sometimes, I lie in bed and try to imagine how it will be when I grow up. My mom says not to worry, and she talks about soulmates finding each other, like dad and she did. How can she say that when my mom and dad fight a lot? Oh, well, I guess I should leave some of the future for the future.

What do I want most to remember about being a kid once I am an adult?

What's the most important advice I want to be able to give adults?

What are some important things for grown-ups to remember?

LOOKING GOOD, FEELING GOOD

Chapter Sixteen

Dancing

Today I was up in my room, dancing to a rock 'n' roll song on the radio. I was getting so hot and sweaty and ready to go wild. It felt so good. My mom came to the door and suddenly opened it. I thought she would get mad at me because my room was a mess, and I was in bare feet, which she hates. But instead, she grinned and came in and actually started dancing with me. She even took a fake long stem rose and held it between her teeth like they do in movies when the woman is dancing the tango. I couldn't believe it. We danced like crazy for two or more songs, and then she collapsed on my bed and pulled me down with her and we hugged. She looked happier than I've seen her in ages.

She told me that she used to dance in her bedroom when she was a kid and she would hold her hairbrush like a microphone and pretend to sing. I was so happy today. I hope we dance together again soon.

As far as what I'm telling you about life I hope that my day today will be a message to you. No matter what comes your way with your parents or your siblings or friends for school work remember that miracles can happen and things can get better and sometimes it just takes waiting a while. Sometimes it takes having an opportunity to try something in a new way. Sometimes it takes just making new friends or letting time pass. It can be easy sometimes and hard other times..

I can't give you advice on everything and I can't give you every example so I want to leave you with a sense of hope and courage and being yourself. Be your true self with your talents and your traits and your wishes and dreams about life. I can't tell you that everything will come great but you will have many happy days and I hope you'll see that life can be wonderful as you dance your tango. Bye for now. I'll be back again when I'm a bit older and have more to share with you about life.

About Dr. Barbara Becker Holstein

Dr. Barbara Becker Holstein, internationally known Positive Psychologist is the creator of The Enchanted Self®, a positive psychology method for happiness and a pioneer in Selfies as Film. Dr. Holstein's Enchanted Self website, EnchantedSelf.com, was included as one of the best websites in positive psychology. She is in private practice in Long Branch, New Jersey with her husband, Dr. Russell M. Holstein.

Dr. Barbara can be found on the web, interviewed, writing articles and posting video 'TED' style talks on happiness, Positive Psychology, relationships and parenting. Her Roku channel is: The Enchanted Self Presents.

She has been a contributor to Your Tango, Heart and Soul, The Philadelphia Inquirer, Honey Good, Cosmopolitan Magazine, Redbook, Real Simple, Women's World, The Wall Street Journal, Psych central.com, Time online, the Today Show and Family Circle Magazine.

Also By Dr. Barbara Becker Holstein

Visit Dr. Holstein's main site at https://enchantedself.com.

BOOKS FOR GIRLS

THE TRUTH SERIES FOR GIRLS

The Truth: Diary of a Gutsy Tween
Published by Sky Horse Press
https://www.skyhorsepublishing.com/

Secrets: Diary of a Gutsy Teen
Published by Sky Horse Press
https://www.skyhorsepublishing.com/

Conflict and a Bit of Magic

DR. BARBARA BECKER HOLSTEIN

A SAMPLING OF OTHER BOOKS FOR WOMEN

Recipes for Enchantment, The Secret Ingredient is YOU!

THE ENCHANTED SELF, a Positive Therapy

Seven Gateways to Happiness: Freeing Your Enchanted Self

7 Ways to Help Your Family Recover From the Pandemic

Next Year In Jerusalem: Around Every Corner, Mystery and Romance

A SAMPLING OF HER FILMS, ALL DESIGNED TO HELP GIRLS COME OF AGE IN HEALTHY WAYS:
Many of her films for girls can be found at
https://rebrand.ly/leythso

Lock Down:

Lock Down Trailer

The Truth A Short Film:

Secrets A Coming Of Age Selfie Film:

Falling In Love A Coming Of Age Selfie Film:

Truth is Stranger Than Fiction:

Truths Change And Still Remain:

Conflict:

Angst:

Selfie:

The Medium, A Coming of Age, Selfie Film:

The Selfie Project Pilot:

Conflict and a Bit of Magic, A Coming of Age, Selfie Film:

DR. HOLSTEIN'S FILMS, ZOOM DRAMAS AND PRESENTATIONS FOR ADULTS CAN BE FOUND AT

https://vimeo.com/showcase/6832893

www.ingramcontent.com/pod-product-compliance
Lightning Source LLC
Chambersburg PA
CBHW072213070526
44585CB00015B/1321